My Trip To The Beach

By Kelly Emrick MBA, Ph.D.

My Last Day Of School

Summer Has Arrived

We Are Going To The Beach For Vacation!

Dreaming About The Beach

Packing For Vacation

Getting Excited About Trip

Packing Car For Vacation

Driving To The Beach: Stops Along The Way!

Stopping For Restroom

Stopping For Food

Stopping To Let Skippy Walk

Stopping At My Grandparent's House

Stopping Again At The Restroom

I Drank Too Much Water!

Falling Asleep In The Car

Stopping For Gas Again

Arriving At The Hotel

We Made It To The Beach!

Putting On Sun Blocker

Before Going To Beach

Running To The Beach

Parents Putting-up Umbrella

My Family Swimming

Be Safe. Put On Floaties!

Putting On My Swim Mask

Playing In The Waves

Inflating My Raft

Building A Sandcastle

Putting Water Around The Sandcastle

Getting Buried In Sand

Taking Pictures

Finding Seashells

Feeding The Seagulls

Flying A Kite

Eating Snacks

Playing With The Turtles

Chasing Sand Crabs

Playing With The Dolphins

Relaxing On The Beach

Playing Frisbee

Running On The Beach

Playing Volleyball

Drinking Lots Of Water

Playing Beach Ball

Just Having Fun

Sleeping On The Beach

Paddle Boarding

Canoeing

Riding A Jet Ski

Parasailing

Finding New Friends

Playing With My New Friends

Washing Off Sand

Playing At The Pool

Going Down The Water Slide

Getting Too Much Sun

Going To Amusement Park

Playing Miniature Golf

Jumping On The Bouncy House

Eating Cotton Candy

Riding The Ferris Wheel

Eating Ice-cream

Eating Popcorn

I Ate Too Much

Time For Bed

Early Morning Walk On The Beach

Time To Go Home

The Best Vacation Ever!

Coloring Book Of Things You May See At The Beach

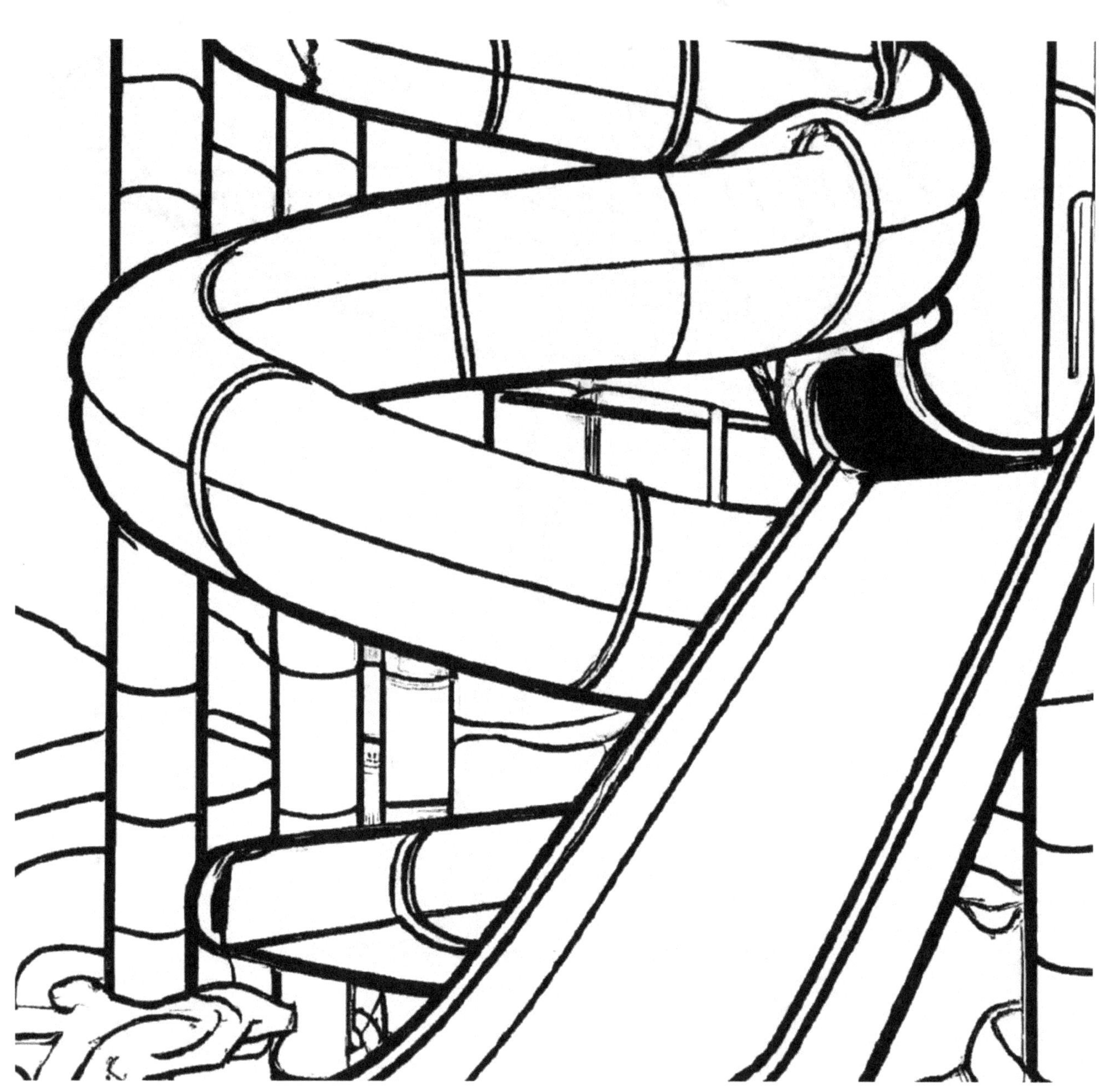

www.ingramcontent.com/pod-product-compliance
Lightning Source LLC
LaVergne TN
LVHW080555160826
845677LV00010B/1856
9798370288586